The Secret of Intercession

Andrew Murray

First published in 1914 by Morgan & Scott Ltd

Note: while the original material is public domain, the modern translation of it is NOT and is copyright of Pastor Joe Lighthall, 2025. All rights reserved.

Permission is required for reuse, reproduction, or distribution of this translated edition.

ISBN 978-1-918219-48-7

This Edition first published: December 2025

Published by: Cosmic Jive Publishing
www.cosmicjivepublishing.com

For permissions and inquiries, contact:
info@cosmicjivepublishing.com

ABOUT THIS EDITION

Andrew Murray's books remain treasures of Christian devotion, yet for many of today's readers they are hard to read. His rich vocabulary, lengthy sentences, long paragraphs, and occasional use of words that have now fallen out of everyday English can create a real barrier—even for those who grew up speaking the language and have studied theology.

This new edition is not an attempt to "improve" Murray (his spiritual insight needs no improvement). It is simply an effort to clear away the obstacles that keep so many from hearing him clearly.

At times a single sentence packs so much into itself that the thought feels knotted. At other times a vital truth lies hidden behind phrasing that no longer carries its original force. When those knots are loosened and those veils lifted, something wonderful happens: Murray's teaching is not only understandable—it is gripping, deeply practical, and profoundly moving.

The moment the meaning breaks through, you understand why his books have been loved for generations. His vision of intercession is not dry doctrine; it is a living invitation to stand alongside Christ Himself in prayer. He presents prayer not as a duty or ritual but as the very channel through which God's blessing flows, the place where He reshapes our hearts and employs us to bring heaven's purposes to earth.

The Secret of Intercession

Murray wrote with a rare combination of humility, passion, and spiritual authority that still feels fresh today—an authority unmistakably forged in a lifetime of communion with God. When his words are set free in clear, contemporary English, their light shines even more brightly.

My earnest hope is that this modernized edition will remove the veil for many who long to drink deeply from Murray's wisdom but have felt shut out before by the language of a bygone era.

May these pages stir in you a fresh hunger for prayer, a stronger confidence in Christ's unending intercession, and a renewed sense of privilege—that you and I are called to partner with God in seeing His kingdom come through the sacred work of intercession.

Pastor Joe Lighthall, 2025

A Note from the Editor

Every chapter, every section, every biblical quotation is here in the same order as the original. Nothing has been removed, added, or softened. What has changed is only the presentation:

- The Victorian-era language has been carefully rewritten in clear, contemporary English so today's readers can immediately grasp Murray's full message.
- Roman numerals have been replaced with ordinary numbers.
- Long, dense paragraphs have been broken into shorter ones for modern eyes
- Some Bible quotations are retained in the wording Murray himself used, because those precise shades of meaning matter.

The meaning, the challenge, and the power of the original words remain exactly the same — only now they are easier to read, to share and to apply.

Introduction

This little book has been written to wake up Christians to a true understanding of the serious duty, the high privilege, and the amazing power of intercession.

It aims to show the place that intercession holds in God's plan for spreading His kingdom and for strengthening the lives of His children, so that they can receive the heavenly blessings that He wants to give them and then pass those blessings on to the world around them.

The original Dutch version has proved very helpful in encouraging Christians to grasp their high calling and in helping them take their proper place among the Lord's "remembrancers" who call upon Him day and night.

This English translation is sent out with the hope and prayer that it will be used in Bible classes and prayer meetings to nurture the spirit of devotion and prayer that is so vital to the Christian life.

A.M.

First Day
Intercession

"Pray one for another."
—Jas. v. 16.

Prayer is a great and glorious mystery! On the one side, we see God in His holiness, love, and power, waiting and longing to bless man. On the other side we see sinful man – a mere worm of the dust – yet one who is able through prayer to draw down from God the very life and love of heaven to live in his own heart.

But the glory of intercession is even greater than the glory of prayer.

Intercession is when a person boldly dares to tell God what he wants for others. It's when he seeks to bring down upon one soul, or maybe upon hundreds and thousands of souls, the power of the eternal life with all its blessings.

Intercession is the holiest expression of our boldness as God's children.

Intercession is the highest privilege and joy in our relationship with God.

Intercession is the power of being used by God as instruments in His great work - His great work being making human beings His dwelling-place and a place to display His glory to the world.

You would expect the Church to consider intercession as one of the main ways that God works in and moves among His people and mankind. (But it doesn't).

You'd also expect the church to seek above all else to cultivate in its members, God's children, the power of an unceasing prayerfulness for a lost and perishing world. (But it doesn't).

You would expect that believers who have begun to understand this secret would feel the strength that comes from unity and the certainty that God will indeed avenge His own chosen ones who cry to Him day and night. (But for the most part, they don't).

The Church will only put on her beautiful garments and her strength when Christians stop looking for help in external union and instead are all bound together to the throne of God by unceasing devotion to Jesus Christ and unceasing prayer for the power of God's Spirit.

Then the church will overcome the world.

Prayer

Our gracious Father,

Hear our prayer and teach Your Church – teach every one of us – what the glory, the blessing, and the all-prevailing power of intercession really are.

Give us the vision of what intercession means to You, that it is essential to carry out Your blessed purpose.

Give us the vision of what it means for us to be acting out our roles as royal priests.

Give us the vision of what it will mean for Your Church and for the lost who are dying without you when the Spirit is poured out in power – for Jesus' sake.

Amen.

Second Day
The Opening of the Eyes

"And Elisha prayed and said: Lord, open his eyes, that he may see ... And Elisha said, Lord, open the eyes of these men, that they may see."
—2 Kings 6:17, 20

Elisha's prayer for his servant was answered wonderfully! The young man saw the mountain full of chariots of fire and horsemen surrounding Elisha. God had sent the armies of heaven to protect His servant.

A second time Elisha prayed. The Syrian army had been struck with blindness and led into Samaria. There Elisha prayed again that their eyes might be opened – and suddenly they saw they were helpless prisoners in the power of their enemy.

We want to use these two prayers in the spiritual realm of the Spirit to help us see.

First, we ask that our own eyes may be

opened to see the astonishing provision God has made for His Church in the baptism with the Holy Spirit and with fire.

All the powers of the heavenly world have been placed at our disposal for the service of Christ's kingdom. Yet how few of God's children live in the faith of that heavenly vision – how few of them believing that the power of the Holy Spirit is really on them, with them, and in them, both for their own spiritual life and as their strength to witness joyfully for their Lord and His work!

But we also need that second prayer of Elisha. We must ask God to have our eyes opened to see the power that the world and sin still have over God's people.

Many believers are still unaware of how weak the Church really is, how powerless she has become to win souls for Christ and to build up believers to live lives of holiness and fruitfulness.

Let us pray especially that God will open everyone's eyes to see the huge need the church is in. That people will see the one huge and basic need of the Church today is to unite together and to intercede to bring down God's blessing.

Let us pray that people will see this kind of intercession among them so the power of God's Spirit is constantly known in all its power and blessing.

Prayer:

Our Father in heaven,

You who are so willing beyond all words to give us the Holy Spirit in power, so hear our humble prayer.

Open our eyes, we beg You.

Let us see clearly both the low condition of Your Church and people, and the unlimited treasures of grace and power You are ready to pour out in answer to the fervent prayer of a united Church.

Amen.

Third Day
Man's Place in God's Plan

"The heaven, even the heavens, are the Lord's; but the earth hath He given to the children of men."
—Psalm 115:16

God created heaven as His own dwelling-place — perfect, glorious, and completely holy. The earth He gave to man as his dwelling-place. Everything was very good, yet only as a beginning that needed to be worked on, kept and cultivated.

The work that God had started, man was to carry forward and perfect.

Think of the iron and coal hidden deep in the earth, of the steam hidden in water. God left it to man to discover these things and put them to use. That is why we now have railways covering the earth and steamships crossing the oceans. God created everything with that use in mind, but He made the discovery and the application depend on man's wisdom, hard work and efforts.

What the earth has become today – its cities, houses, cornfields, and orchards – it owes entirely to man. The work God began and prepared was carried out by human beings in fulfilment of God's purpose.

Nature itself teaches us the amazing partnership into which God invites man in order to complete the work of creation so creation reaches its destiny.

This same law holds true in the kingdom of grace. In the great redemption, God has revealed the power of the heavenly life and the spiritual blessings that heaven overflows with. Yet His redeemed people have been entrusted with the task of making these blessings known to others and bringing others to share in them.

The children of this world eagerly seek the treasures hidden in the earth that God has hidden for their use. In the same way, God's children should be just as eager, diligent and faithful in seeking the treasures stored in heaven and bringing them down to bless the world.

It is through the unceasing intercession

of God's people that God's Kingdom comes and His will is done on earth as in heaven.

Prayer:

Ever-blessed Lord,
How wonderful is the role you have given man, entrusting him to continue Your work that You have started.
We ask you to open our hearts to understand the amazing thought that through the preaching of the gospel and through the work of intercession that Your people work out Your purpose.
Lord, Open our eyes—for Jesus' sake.
Amen.

FOURTH DAY
Intercession in the Plan of Redemption

> "O You who hear prayer, to You all flesh will come."
> — Psalm 65:2

When God made man in His image and gave him dominion, it was so man would be His appointed ruler on earth.

It was His plan that Adam would do nothing but with God and through God. It was God's plan that God Himself would do all His work in the world through Adam.

Man really did possess the authority to be the owner, master, and ruler of the earth - legally having being given the deeds of entitlement to this from God.

When sin entered the world, Adam's power was proved to be a terrible reality, for through him the earth, with the whole human race, was brought under a curse.

When God made the plan of redemption,

His purpose was to restore man to his original place. He chose servants of old who, through the power of intercession, could ask for whatever they wanted and it would be given them

When Christ became man, it was that—as man—He might intercede for humanity both on heaven and on earth.

In His Farewell Discourse (John 14–17), which was given to his disciples before He left this world, Jesus gave His disciples the same right of intercession in His seven-part promise. The promise that whatsoever they should ask, He would do it for them.

God's intense longing to bless is, in a sense, graciously limited by His dependence on man's intercession rising from earth. He seeks to awaken the spirit of intercession so He may pour out His blessing on mankind.

God views intercession as the highest demonstration of His people's readiness to receive His power and to wholly submit themselves to the working of His mighty power.

Christians must realize that as royal priests and as children of the king that their only power with God is the right to claim the things asked for and to expect that God will hear their prayer.

Only when believers grasp what intercession means for God's Kingdom will they understand their own serious part to play and their own responsibility.

Every single believer will be led to see that God waits for him to take his place, to fulfil his role, to do his job.

Intercession—day and night pleading with God that heaven's power be sent down and descend into human hearts—is the most blessed and powerful human tool for fulfilling the plea; "on earth as in heaven."

May God impress this on us and burn it on our hearts: intercession, with its omnipotent power, is according to His will and is truly effective.

FIFTH DAY
God Seeks Intercessors

"He saw that there was no man, and was amazed that there was no intercessor."
— Isaiah 59:16

From ancient times, God had intercessors among His people whose prayers He listened to and whose prayers brought deliverance for the people.

But here, we read of a time He looked for an intercessor but in vain—there was none. He *was amazed*. Imagine that—God astonished that no one loved the people enough, or trusted in His power enough to deliver His people.

Nobody loved or trusted God enough to intercede and plead for the people.

If someone had stood in the gap as an intercessor, God would have given deliverance.

Without an intercessor, his judgments came down (Isaiah 64:7; Ezekiel 22:30–31).

What immense and eternal importance God places on the role of the intercessor in the kingdom of God!

Isn't it amazing that God gives men such power, and yet that there are so few people who know what it is to take hold of God's strength and pray down His blessing on the world ? What a tragedy!

When Christ completed His work on earth and ascended to His throne in heaven, He entrusted man with the task of advancing His Kingdom.

Christ lives forever to pray, and intercession is the highest expression of His royal authority as the Priest-King on the throne.

All that Christ was to do in heaven was to be in fellowship with His people on earth. In His wisdom, God has willed and decreed that the working of His Spirit should follow the prayers of His people.

He waits for their intercession.

He waits for His people to prepare their hearts to intercede.

He waits for His people to receive His

spirit as much as they are ready to receive.

He rules the world and His Church through the prayers of His saints.

That God should have made the growth of His Kingdom to such a large extent dependent on the faithfulness of His people in prayer is a stupendous mystery and yet also an absolute certainty.

God calls for intercessors : in His grace He has made His work dependent on them; He waits for them.

Prayer:

Father,
Open our eyes to see Your invitation to have a share in growing Your Kingdom through faithful prayer and intercession.

Give us such a vision of this holy calling that we may yield ourselves wholly to this blessed task.

Amen.

SIXTH DAY
Christ as Intercessor

"He is able to save them to the uttermost that come unto God by Him, seeing He ever liveth to make intercession for them"
— Hebrews 7:25

After God said in Isaiah that He was amazed that there was no intercessor, He then said: "Therefore His arm brought salvation unto Him. The Redeemer shall come to Zion".

Because God found no intercessor, He Himself provided one—Christ, His Son (Isaiah 59:16, 20; 53:12).

God Himself would provide the true intercessor, in Christ of whom it had already been said : "He bare the sin of many, and made intercession for the transgressors"

Jesus began his work as an intercessor on earth. Think of His high-priestly prayer on behalf of His disciples and all who would believe through them. His words to Peter—"I have prayed for you"—show how personal His intercession is. Even on the cross He spoke as an intercessor: "Father, forgive them."

Now, seated at God's right hand, He continues this work of intercession unceasingly as our great High Priest. But with this difference, *that* He gives His people power to take part in it.

He promised seven times in His Farewell Discourse (in John) that what they asked Him to do, He would do. The power of heaven was to be at their disposal. This was a promise.

Heaven's power stands at the disposal of those who pray. That's a promise.

But the grace and power of God waits for men to ask.

The leading of the Holy Spirit teaches people God's will.

Faith enables them to pray in Christ's name.

Christ presents their prayers to the Father, and through His and His people's united intercession the Church receives the

Spirit's power and is clothed in it.

Prayer:

Blessed Redeemer,
What amazing grace—that You call us to share in Your intercession!
We ask you to awaken in Your redeemed people an awareness of the glory of this calling.
We ask you to awaken in your people an awareness of the rich blessing which your Church in its impotence can, through its intercession in your name, bring down upon this earth.
May the Holy Spirit work in hearts and deeply Convict us of the sin of restrained prayer, of the laziness and unbelief and selfishness that is the cause of this lack of activity.
May the Holy Spirit convince us of your loving desire to pour out the Spirit of prayer in answer to the requests, and from all, for your name's sake.
AMEN.

SEVENTH DAY
The Intercessors God Seeks

"I have set watchmen upon Thy walls, O Jerusalem ; they shall never hold their peace day nor night: ye that are the Lord's remembrancers, take ye no rest and give Him no rest."
— Isaiah 62:6–7

Watchmen are usually placed on a city's walls to advance-warn the leaders of the city of pending danger. God appoints His watchmen not only to warn people (who often don't listen)—but also to summon Him to act for them whenever need or danger threatens.

The great sign of interceding watchmen is this: they do not keep silent; they do not rest day and night; and they do not allow God to rest either until deliverance comes.

They may be confident and have faith that God will answer. Christ said, "Will not

God bring justice to His chosen ones who cry to Him day and night?"

Everywhere in the world today we hear that the Church, influenced by worldly power and the earthly-mindedness that worldliness brings, is losing its influence over its members.

Very few sinners are converted under God's power, few believers walk in holiness, there is little experience of the power of the Holy Spirit, and the great majority of Christians utterly neglect Christ's call to help grow His Kingdom.

Amid all the discussion about how to interest young and old in the study of God's Word, or to rekindle love for the church's services, one rarely hears of the essential need for the Holy Spirit's power in the pulpit and in the pews alike.

One sees little sign of the conviction or confession that the weakness of the Spirit's working is due to our lack of prayer, and that only through united, fervent, passionate prayer can anything be changed.

If ever there was a time when God's people should cry to Him day and night, it is now.

Will you offer yourself to God for this blessed work of intercession, and learn to count it the highest privilege of your life to be a channel through whose prayers God's blessing can come down to earth?

Prayer:

Ever-blessed Father,

Hear us, we pray, and raise up the intercessors You desire.

Give us, we ask, men and women who will stand before You as Your remembrancers—taking no rest and giving You no rest until Your Church becomes a praise in the earth again.

Blessed Father, let Your Spirit teach us how to pray.

Amen.

EIGHTH DAY
The School of Intercession

"In the days of His flesh, He offered up prayers and supplications with loud cries and tears... and was heard."
— Hebrews 5:7

Christ is the Intercessor in heaven; we, His Body, share His work as partners with Him on earth. Let no one think it cost Jesus nothing to become an intercessor. Isaiah says He poured out His soul unto death— three times repeating that phrase (Isaiah 53:10–12).

"When Thou shalt make *His soul an offering for sin,* He shall see His seed ... .

He shall see of the *travail of His soul . .. .I will divide Him a portion with the great,* because *He hath poured out His soul unto death."*

This pouring out of the soul is God's definition of intercession. This intercession give His sacrifice and prayer their power with God

His giving Himself to live and die for the salvation of the perishing was a revelation of the very spirit that has power to prevail with God..

If we as helpers and fellow-labourers with the Lord Jesus are to share Christ's power of intercession, we too must experience something of His soul's travail—giving up our lives and pleasures for the urgent work of pleading for others.

Intercession must not be occasional; it must become a growing passion we are intense about that shapes our lives of consecration and sacrifice.

It is a life of consecration and self-sacrifice that truly gives power for intercession (Acts 15:26; 20:24; Phil. 2:17; Rev. 12:11).

The more we study this blessed truth and consider what it means to exercise this power for God's glory and the salvation of people, the deeper our conviction will grow that it is worth giving up everything to share with Christ in His work of intercession.

Prayer:

Blessed Lord Jesus,
Teach us to join You in calling upon God for the souls You have purchased.
Fill us with Your love, fill the rest of your church with your love, that we may plead for the Spirit's power to be revealed.
Amen.

NINTH DAY
The Name of Jesus: the Power of Intercession

"Until now you have asked nothing in My name... Ask, and you will receive, so that your joy may be full."
— John 16:24, 26

During Christ's earthly ministry, His disciples knew little of prayer's power. In Gethsemane, Peter and the others failed completely. They did not yet understand what it meant to ask in Jesus' name and receive.

But Jesus promised that in the coming day that was coming they would pray with such power in His name that whatever they asked for would be given.

"Hitherto nothing."

"In that day ye shall ask in My name and shall receive."

Even now these two conditions are seen

in the Church: the great majority of Christians scarcely understand their oneness with Christ or the Spirit's work as the Spirit of prayer, and therefore never attempting to claim Christ's wonderful promises Christ gives here.

But those of God's children who know what it is to abide in Christ and in vital union to Him, and yield to the Spirit's leading and teaching, begin to understand and experience the effectiveness of their intercession.

They see their intercession achieves a lot, and that God will give the power of His Spirit in answer to their prayer

Faith in the power of Jesus' name—and in our right to use it—gives us the courage to follow to where God invites us to act in the holy role of intercessors.

When our Lord Jesus, in His Farewell Discourse, gave His unlimited prayer promise, He sent the disciples into the world with this assurance and awareness: "He who sits upon the throne, and who lives in my heart, has promised that what I ask in His name I shall receive. *He will do it.*"

If Christians only knew what it is to yield

themselves wholly and absolutely to Jesus Christ and His service. Their eyes would be opened to see that intense, unceasing prayer is the essential mark of a healthy spiritual life.

They'd see that the power of prevailing intercession will indeed belong to those who live only in, and for, their Lord.

Prayer:

Blessed Saviour,
Grant us the Holy Spirit's grace to live in You and with you and for You, so that we may boldly believe our prayers are heard.
Amen.

TENTH DAY
Prayer: the Work of the Spirit

"God has sent the Spirit of His Son into our hearts, crying, 'Abba, Father.'"
— Galatians 4:6

We know what "Abba, Father" meant for Jesus in Gethsemane: complete surrender to death so that God's redeeming will could be accomplished.

In His prayer, He was ready for any sacrifice including giving his life. That prayer of His reveals to us the heart of the One now interceding in heaven at the right hand of God. In that place with the wonderful power of intercession that He exercises there, and the power to pour down the Holy Spirit.

The Holy Spirit has been given by the Father to breathe this same Spirit of Jesus into our hearts, so that we surrender ourselves to God's will as fully as Jesus did and to pray like Jesus did that His love be fulfilled on earth—at any cost.

Just as God's love is revealed in His desire for the salvation of souls, so the desire of Jesus was made plain when He gave Himself for them.

Jesus asks that His love for souls become ours, should fill us, so we give ourselves wholly to intercession and, at all costs, pray down God's love upon the perishing.

And lest we fear this demand is too much or the cost is too high, the Spirit of Jesus is given to enable us to pray in Christ's likeness, in His name and in His power.

Those who yield fully to the Spirit will feel the divine compulsion of love urging them into a life of continual intercession, because the one who does it knows that it is God who is working in him.

Now we can understand how Christ could give His disciples such unlimited promises of answered prayer: they were first to be filled with the Holy Spirit.

And now we see how God can give intercession such a high place in fulfilling His purpose of redemption: it is the Holy

Spirit who breathes God's own desire into us and enables us to intercede for souls.

Prayer:

"Abba, Father"
Grant that through Your Holy Spirit we will keep up unceasing intercession for the souls for whom Christ died.

Give to your children the vision of the blessings and the power which come to those who yield themselves to this high calling.

Amen

ELEVENTH DAY
Christ Our Example in Intercession

> *"He shall divide the spoil with the strong, because ... He bare the sin of many and made intercession for the transgressors."*
> — Isaiah 53:12

"He made intercession for the transgressors." What did that mean to Him? Think of what it cost Him to pray that prayer effectually

Consider what it meant for Christ to intercede for sinners. To pray effectively, He had to pour out His soul as an offering for sin and to cry in Gethsemane : "Father, Thy holy will of love be done."

Think what moved Him to sacrifice Himself to the very uttermost! It was His love for the Father—that the Father's holiness might be revealed—and His love for souls, that they might share in that holiness.

His love for the Father and for souls moved Him to this extreme sacrifice.

His reward was glorious: defeating every enemy, seated now at God's right hand, He now exercises limitless and assured intercession.

And Jesus desires a people, a generation of those who share His same mind, whom He can train to share in His great work of intercession.

To intercede like Him, we must yield ourselves completely to God's holiness and love, saying, "Your will be done, whatever it costs," even if it means pouring out our life unto death.

Jesus truly brings us into a partnership with Himself. He takes us up into it in carrying out the great work of intercession.

He in heaven and we on earth must share one purpose, one mind, one aim: from love for the Father and the lost, we consecrate our lives to intercession for God's blessing.

The burning desire of Father and Son for the salvation of souls must be the burning desire of our hearts too.

What an honor and what a blessing ...

and what a power for us to do the work—because He lives and pours His love into our hearts through the Spirit!

Prayer:

Everlasting God of love,
Open our eyes to the vision of the glory of Your Son who ever lives to pray.
Open our eyes to the glory of the grace that enables us in His likeness to also live and intercede for sinners.
Father, for Jesus' sake.
AMEN.

TWELFTH DAY
God's Will and Ours

"Your will be done."
— Matthew 26:42

God's highest prerogative is that His will is done everywhere—in heaven and on earth; that everything everywhere is done according to His will and as the fulfilment of His desires.

When He made man in His image, God intended that human desires align perfectly with His own. This is man's high honor of being in the likeness of God: to desire what God desires, to feel and wish just as God.

Man was to be the embodiment and fulfilment of God's desires in human flesh.

But when God gave man the power to choose, He also limited Himself in the exercise of His will.

After the fall, man had fallen and yielded himself to the will of God's enemy. Man's desires centred on earthly things. Then God, in his infinite love, went to work to win man back, to restore man so that man's desires become His desires again.

As with God, so with man—desire is the great driving power. And since man had given himself over to desiring the things of earth and the flesh, God had to redeem him and train him into a life in harmony with Himself.

His one aim was that human desire should come into perfect agreement with His own.

The great step toward this was taken when the Son of the Father came into the world to reproduce the desires of God within His human nature, and in prayer to yield Himself to the perfect fulfilment of all that God desired and willed.

As Man, the Son said in agony and blood, "Thy will be done," and made the surrender —even to being forsaken by God—so that the power that had deceived humanity might be conquered and deliverance secured.

It was through the wonderful and complete harmony between the Father and the Son—when the Son said, "Thy will of love be done"—that the great redemption was accomplished.

And this is now the great work in making that redemption our own: that believers must say, first for themselves and then in lives devoted to intercession for others, "Thy will be done on earth as it is in heaven."

Now we must appropriate this redemption by praying first for ourselves, and then for others in intercession: "Your will be done on earth as in heaven."

As we pray for for the Church-ministers, missionaries, its strong Christians or its young converts, and as we pray for the unsaved, whether nominally Christian or heathen, we have the privilege of pleading for what God Himself wants—and through our prayers, His will is done on earth as in heaven.

THIRTEENTH DAY
The Blessedness of a Life of Intercession

> "You who are the Lord's remembrancers, take no rest and give Him no rest, until He makes Jerusalem a praise in the earth."
> —Isaiah 62:6-7

What indescribable grace—that we are allowed to deal with God in intercession for the needs of others!

What a blessing, to be in close union with Christ and sharing in His great work as Intercessor and to mingle our prayers with His!

What an honor it is to have power and influence with God in heaven on behalf of souls, and to obtain for them what they do not yet know what to ask for and cannot even imagine!

What a privilege to be a steward of God's grace, to bring before Him the condition of the Church or of individual souls and to plead for them on their behalf until God entrusts us with the answer!

Whether these people we plead for are God's ministers, or His messengers in distant lands, what a privilege!

What a blessing to be in fellowship with other children of God, and to labor together with them in prayer until victory is gained —whether over earthly difficulties or obstacles or over the powers of darkness in high places!

It is really worth living for: knowing that God will use me as an intercessor— receiving and distributing His heavenly blessing here on earth, and above all, the power of His Holy Spirit.

This is, in reality, the life of heaven—it is the life of the Lord Jesus Himself. In His self-denying love, He takes possession of me and urges me to yield myself wholly too so that I carry the burden of souls before Him, and to plead that they may live.

For too long we have thought of prayer only as a way to supply our own needs in life and for service. May God help us to see the place intercession holds in His divine plan and in His work for the Kingdom.

And may our hearts truly feel that no honor or earthly blessing compares with the unspeakable privilege of waiting upon God and bringing down from heaven the blessing that He delights to give—and the blessing of opening the way on earth for that blessing to flow.

Prayer:

Oh my Father,
Let Your life truly flow down to this earth and fill the hearts of Your children.
As the Lord Jesus pours out His love in His unceasing intercession in heaven, let it be so with us here on earth: a life of overflowing love and never-ending intercession.
Amen.

FOURTEENTH DAY
The Place of Prayer

"These all continued with one accord in prayer and supplication."
—Acts 1:14

The last words Christ spoke before He left the world give us the four great messages for His Church to note:

1. "Wait for the promise of the Father."

2. "You shall receive power when the Holy Spirit has come upon you."

3. "You shall be witnesses unto Me."

4. "Both in Jerusalem and to the ends of the earth."

These are the signs of the true Gospel, the

true ministry, and the true New Testament Church: united and unceasing prayer, the power of the Holy Spirit, and living witnesses to the living Christ from Jerusalem to the uttermost part of the earth.

A Church of united, unceasing prayerfulness; a ministry filled with the Holy Spirit; members who are living witnesses of a living Christ, carrying His message to every person on earth—*this* was the Church Christ founded, and this was the Church that went out to conquer the world.

After Christ ascended to heaven, the disciples immediately knew what their work must be: to continue together, with one accord, in prayer and supplication.

The disciples were to be bound into one body by the love and Spirit of Christ. This unity gave them great power—power in heaven with God, and power on earth among people.

The disciples' one duty was to wait in united and unceasing prayer for the Holy Spirit's power—the power from on high that would equip them to witness for Christ to the ends of the earth.

A praying Church, a Spirit-filled Church, a witnessing Church—embracing the whole world as its mission—*this* is the Church of Jesus Christ.

As long as the Church maintained this character, the church had power to conquer. But unfortunately, as it came under the influence of the world, it lost so much of its heavenly, supernatural beauty and strength.

How unfaithful the church became in prayer, how feeble the church became in the workings of the Spirit, how insipid its witness to Christ, and how unfaithful to its worldwide mission it was!

Prayer:

Blessed Lord Jesus,
Have mercy on Your Church.
Give us, we pray, the Spirit of prayer and supplication as in the days of old, so that Your Church may again prove, show and demonstrate the power that comes from You and bear witness to You in winning the world to come to kneel at Your feet.
Amen.

FIFTEENTH DAY
Paul as an Intercessor

"I bow my knees to the Father, that He would grant you to be strengthened with power through His Spirit."
—Ephesians 3:14, 16

We think of Paul as the great missionary, the great preacher, the great writer, the great apostle—"in labors more abundant."

But we do not think enough of Paul as the intercessor—the one who, through prayer, sought and received the divine strength that empowered all his other work, and brought down the blessing that rested on the churches he served.

We see above what he writes to the Ephesians. Consider also what he says to the Thessalonians (1 Thessalonians 3:10, 13):

"Night and day praying exceedingly, that we might perfect that which is lacking in your faith, to the end He may stablish your hearts unblameable in holiness."

To the Romans Paul says (1:9):

"Without ceasing I make mention of you always in my prayers."

To the Philippians (1:4):

"Always in every prayer of mine for you all, making my requests with joy."

And to the Colossians (1:9; 2:1):

"We do not cease to pray for you. I would that ye knew what great conflict I have for you."

Day and night, Paul cried out to God in intercession for these people, that the light and power of the Holy Spirit might rest upon them. And just as strongly as he believed in the power of his prayers for them, he believed in the blessing their prayers would bring upon him.

"I beseech you, that ye strive together with me in your prayers to God for me" — Romans 15:30

"God will yet deliver us, ye also helping together by prayer for us " —2 Corinthians 1:10-11

"Praying also for me, that I may open my mouth boldly." —Ephesians 6:18-19;

Colossians 4:3; 2 Thessalonians 3:1

"This shall turn to my salvation through your prayer." —Philippians 1:19

The entire relationship between pastor and people depends on united, continual prayerfulness. Their whole connection with each other is spiritual and heavenly—and can only be maintained by unceasing prayer.

When ministers and people awaken to the reality that the power and blessing of the Holy Spirit are waiting for their united, persistent prayer, then the Church will begin to understand what Pentecostal, apostolic Christianity truly is.

Prayer:

Ever-blessed Father, we humbly ask You —restore to Your Church the spirit of supplication and intercession.

For Jesus' sake.
Amen.

SIXTEENTH DAY
Intercession for Laborers

"The harvest truly is plentiful, but the laborers are few. Therefore pray to the Lord of the harvest that He will send forth labourers into His harvest."
—Matthew 9:37–38

The disciples did not understood much about what these words meant. Jesus planted them as a seed-thought, to rest in their hearts until the right time.

At Pentecost, as the disciples saw many of the new converts—filled with the Spirit—ready to testify of Christ, they must have recognized how the ten days of united, continual prayer had brought this blessing too: laborers for the harvest, raised up by the Spirit's power.

Christ meant to teach us that no matter how vast the field or how few the workers, prayer is the best, surest, and only real means of meeting the need.

We must understand that the prayer for laborers is not something offered only when the need feels urgent (to us). The entire work is always to be carried forward in a *spirit of prayer*, so that the prayer for laborers is in harmony with all our life and efforts.

In the China Inland Mission, when the number of missionaries had reached 200, a conference in China deeply felt the urgent need for more workers for unreached districts without missionaries or mission bases. After much prayer, they believed they could confidently ask God for 100 additional laborers and £10,000 to support them—within a year. They agreed to continue praying daily throughout that year. When the year ended, the 100 suitable men and women had been found, and £11,000 had been provided.

Throughout the world—its open mission fields and waiting souls—the churches keep complaining of a lack of workers and funds. But doesn't Christ's voice call us back to the united and unceasing prayer of the first disciples?

God is faithful. By the power of His Spirit, He is well able to supply every need. Let the Church take the posture of united prayer and supplication. God hears prayer.

Prayer:

Blessed Lord Jesus,

Teach Your Church what it means to live and work for You in a spirit of unceasing prayerfulness, so that our faith may rise to the assurance that You will—indeed, in ways beyond all expectation—meet the desperate need of a dying world.

Amen.

SEVENTEENTH DAY
Intercession for Individual Souls

"You shall be gathered one by one, O children of Israel." —Isaiah 27:12

In our physical body, each part, each organ, has its appointed place and role. It is the same in society and in the Church. All work must aim for the welfare and perfection of the whole body through the cooperation of every individual member doing their bit.

Yet in the Church, many think the salvation of souls is the minister's work. But the minister usually speaks to the crowd and rarely reaches individuals personally.

This produces a twofold harm and evil:

> **1.** Believers fail to realize that they must personally testify to those around them—to feed them spiritually for their own spiritual

strength and growth and maturity, and for the gathering in of souls into the kingdom.

2. Unconverted people suffer great, unspeakable loss because Christ is not brought to them personally by each believer they encounter.

The thought of intercession for those around us is far too rare. If intercession was restored to its rightful place in Christian life, it would greatly bless the Church and its missionary work.

Oh, when will Christians learn the great truth: "What God in heaven desires to do on earth must have prayer on earth as its essential condition."

When we realize this, we will see that intercession is the chief element in the conversion of souls. All our efforts are powerless without the Holy Spirit, who is given in answer to prayer.

When ministers and people unite in a covenant of prayer and testimony, the Church will flourish, and each believer will understand the part he is meant to play.

What can we do to stir up the spirit of intercession? The answer is twofold:

1. Begin with individuals.

As soon as a Christian begins to understand the need and power of intercession, let him start at once—praying for single souls.

Pray for your children, your relatives, your friends, and all whom God brings across your path.

If you discover that you lack the power to intercede, let that humbling realization drive you to the throne of grace. God desires every redeemed child of His to intercede for the perishing. It is the vital breath of normal Christian life—the evidence that a life is born from above.

2. Pray intensely and persistently for the Spirit's power.

Pray that God will pour out His Holy Spirit upon you and upon His children around you, so that the power of intercession may take the place God intends to honor.

EIGHTEENTH DAY
Intercession for Ministers

"And for me..."
—Ephesians 6:19
"Praying also for us..."
—Colossians 4:3
"Finally, brethren, pray for us."
—2 Thessalonians 3:1

Paul's sayings here show how deeply he was convinced that Christians truly have influence with God, and his faith that their prayers would in reality bring him new strength in his work.

Paul had such a vivid sense of the actual unity of the Body of Christ—of how every member, even the most honored, depends on the life flowing through the *whole* Body—that he stirs believers, for their own sake, for his sake, and for the sake of God's Kingdom, with his appeal: "Continue in prayer, and watch in the same with thanksgiving... praying also for us."

The Church depends on its ministry far more than we often actually realize. The position of the minister is exceedingly high: as a steward of the mysteries of God and as an ambassador pleading with men in Christ's name to be reconciled to Him. If such a minister is unfaithful or lacking in spiritual power, it brings a serious blight upon the Church that the person serves.

If Paul—after preaching for twenty years in the power of God—still needed the prayers of believers, how much more does the ministry today need them!

The minister *needs* the prayers of his people.
* He has a right to them.
* He is truly dependent on them.

It is the minister's task to train Christians for their work of intercession on behalf of the Church and the world. But he must begin by training them to pray for himself. Indeed, he may have to begin even earlier—by learning to pray more earnestly for himself and for them.

Let all intercessors who desire to enter more deeply into their blessed calling give a larger place in their prayers to the ministry —whether for the ministers in their own church or in other churches.

Let them plead with God for individual ministers and for particular groups.

Let them continue in prayer and watchfulness, asking that ministers may be people of power, people of prayer, and people filled with the Holy Spirit.

Pray for the ministry!

Prayer:

Our Father in heaven,
We humbly ask You to awaken believers to their calling to pray in the spirit of faith for the ministers of the Gospel.
Amen.

NINETEENTH DAY
Prayer for All Saints

"With all prayer and supplication praying at all seasons in the Spirit, and watching thereunto with all perseverance and supplication for all the saints."
—Ephesians 6:18 (R.V.)

Notice how Paul repeats his phrases, revealing the intensity of his desire to reach the hearts of his readers:

"All prayer... all seasons... all perseverance... all supplication."

These words call for deep thought if we are to respond as we should.

Paul felt so deeply and profoundly the unity of the Body of Christ, and he was so certain that this unity could only be realized through love and prayer, that he urged the believers in Ephesus—unceasingly and fervently—to pray for all the saints.

The Secret of Intercession

He told them to pray not only for those in their immediate circle, but for all in the Church of Christ whom they heard about.

"Unity is strength." As we exercise the ministry of intercession with perseverance, we will be delivered from self—with its small, weak prayers—and lifted up into a larger heart in which the love of Christ can flow freely and fully through us.

The great lack in so many sincere believers is that in prayer they are occupied with *themselves*—with what God must do for *them*.

Let us realize that here is a call for every believer to give himself continually and unceasingly to the exercise of love and prayer.

It is as we forget ourselves—trusting that God will care for us—and as we give ourselves to the great and blessed work of calling down God's blessing on our brothers and sisters, that the whole Church will be prepared to do its work in making Christ known to every creature.

This alone is the healthy and blessed life of a child of God who has wholly yielded himself to Christ Jesus.

Pray for God's children and for the Church around you.

Pray for all the work in which they are engaged—or ought to be engaged.

Pray at all seasons in the Spirit for all God's saints.

There is no greater blessing than having abiding communion with God, and there is no way that leads to this abiding communion more surely than the life of intercession.

And this is exactly what these words of Paul so passionately call us to.

TWENTIETH DAY
Missionary Intercession

"When they had fasted and prayed, and laid their hands on them, they sent them away."
—Acts 13:3

The biggest question of Foreign Missions is how to multiply the number of Christians —individual and united—who will wield the power of intercession for the conversion and transformation of people,

Every other plan or consideration is secondary to the task of wielding the power of prayer.

We take for granted that all who love this work and carry it on their hearts will obey the Scriptural command to pray unceasingly for the conversion of true converts who become true disciples.

For such people, not only the Morning Watch and hours of regular devotion, but *every* time and season will find them in an attitude of intercession—refusing to let God go until He crowns His workers in the harvest fields with victory.

Missions have their root in the love of Christ—shown on the cross and now living in our hearts. As people labor hard to fulfil God's purpose in the natural world by missionary activity, so God's children should be at least as wholehearted and work just as hard when seeking to bring Christ's love to all humanity through intercession.

Intercession is the chief means God has appointed to make Christ's great work of redemption available to all.

Pray for missionaries, that the life of Christ may be clear and strong in them; that they may be people of prayer, filled with love. Pray for missionaries that they may be people in whom the power of the Holy Spirit is visible and demonstrated.

Pray for Christians living in lands which are predominantly full of unbelievers, that they may know "the glory of this mystery among the heathen: Christ in you, the hope of glory."

Pray for the baptism classes and all the pupils in schools, that the teaching of God's Word may come with power.

Pray especially for the native pastors and evangelists, that the Holy Spirit may fill them to be strong witnesses for Christ among their own people.

Pray, above all, for the whole Church of Christ—that it may be lifted out of its indifference, and that every believer may come to understand that the one purpose of his life is to help make Christ King over all the earth.

Prayer:

Our gracious God,
Our eyes are upon You. Will You not in mercy hear our prayer, and by the Holy Spirit reveal the presence and power of Christ in the work of Your servants?
Amen.

TWENTY-FIRST DAY
The Grace of Intercession

"Continue in prayer, and watch in the same with thanksgiving, withal praying also for us."
—Colossians 4:2–3

Nothing brings us nearer to God or leads us deeper into His love than the work of intercession.

Nothing gives us a greater experience of Christlikeness than the power of pouring out our hearts to His heart, for those around us.

Nothing links us so closely to Jesus Christ —the great Intercessor—or allows us to know His Spirit and power resting on us, as we surrender our lives to the work of bringing the great redemption into the hearts and lives of others.

Nothing reveals more of the mighty working of the Holy Spirit than the prayer

He breathes into our hearts: "Abba, Father," in all the fullness it held for Christ in Gethsemane.

Nothing so helps us demonstrate the power and faithfulness of God to His Word as when we stretch out our intercession to the multitudes—whether within the Church or among the world.

If we pour out our souls before God as a living sacrifice, with this one persistent plea —that He would, in answer to our prayer, open the windows of heaven and send down abundant blessing—then God will be glorified, and our own souls will reach their highest destiny, and His Kingdom will come.

Nothing will help us so much to understand and experience the living unity of the Body of Christ, and the irresistible power it can exert, as daily and continued fellowship with God's people in persistent pleading. Pleading that He would arise, have mercy on Zion, and make the church a light and a life to those sitting in darkness.

How little we realize what we lose by not living in fervent intercession! How little we realize what we may gain—for ourselves and for the world—if we allow God's Spirit, as a Spirit of grace and supplication, to take full possession of our being.

In heaven, Christ lives to pray; His whole communion with the Father is prayer—asking and receiving the fullness of the Spirit for His people.

God delights in nothing so much as prayer.

We should learn to believe that the highest blessings of heaven will unfold to us as we pray more.

Prayer:

Blessed Father,
Pour out the Spirit of supplication and intercession on Your people, for Jesus Christ's sake.
Amen.

TWENTY-SECOND DAY
United Intercession

"There is one body, and one Spirit."
—Ephesians 4:4

Our own physical bodies teach us how essential it is for every one of our body parts to take its full share in seeking the welfare of the whole body. It is the same in the Body of Christ.

Sadly, there are many in the church who think of salvation only in relation to their own happiness.

Others do understand that they are not just to live for themselves. They understand they are to sincerely work and pray to bring others into the same joy they have received. Yet they still do not realize that they are called beyond their personal circle or local church.

These people must understand that they are called to enlarge their hearts—to take the whole Body of Christ Jesus into their love and intercession.

This is precisely what the Spirit and the love of Christ enable us to do.

It is only when intercession for the whole Church, by the whole Church, rises to God's throne that the Spirit of unity and power can exercise His full power.

The growing desire for closer fellowship between the various branches of Christ's Church is something to thank God for. And yet, the difficulties are so great—especially between the different nations and cultures of the world—that the thought of a visibly united Church on earth seems beyond our reach.

Let us thank God that there is a unity in Christ Jesus deeper and stronger than any outward form could ever produce, and that there is a practical way for that unity to be expressed even now.

Despite all our differences, whatever they are, our unity can become a powerful channel of divine strength and blessing for the Kingdom's work.

True unity happens through cultivating and increasing the spirit of intercession and putting that spirit of intercession to work in prayer.

As believers learn what it means to be a *royal priesthood*, they come to see that God is not confined in His love or promises to their small spheres of labor.

He invites them to enlarge their hearts—to pray, like Christ and like Paul, for *all* who already believe, and for all who can yet be brought to believe.

Then the earth and the Church of Christ upon it will, through intercession, be bound to the throne of heaven as never before.

Let Christians and ministers unite together and bind themselves together for this worldwide intercession. This will strengthen the confidence that God hears prayer, and will make their prayers themselves essential for the coming of the Kingdom.

TWENTY-THIRD DAY
Unceasing Intercession

"Pray without ceasing."
—1 Thessalonians 5:17

How different the standard of most Christians is from the standard of scripture; that is the standard which scripture gives us for someone leading a life in the service of God.

For most Christians, the chief concern is their personal safety—to receive grace that pardons sin and to live a life that will secure their own entrance into heaven.

How much higher is the Bible's standard: a Christian fully surrendered, with every ability, every moment, every thought, and every feeling yielded to the glorious God who redeemed them—a God whose fellowship is already the beginning of heaven.

To most Christians, the command "Pray

without ceasing" seems unnecessary and impossible—a requirement of perfection no one can reach.

People wonder: Who can do that? We can get to heaven without it?

But to the true believer, the one following the standards of scripture, the command *pray without ceasing* holds out the promise of the biggest happiness for them—a life crowned with blessings poured out on others through their intercession.

And as the true believer perseveres, it becomes more and more his highest aim on earth, his greatest joy, and his deepest experience of fellowship with the holy God.

"Pray without ceasing!" Let us take that word with a large faith to be a promise of what God's Spirit is willing to work in us, and of how close and intimate our union with the Lord Jesus can be, making us more like Him in His unending intercession at God's right hand.

Let unceasing prayer become one of the chief elements of our heavenly calling: to be consciously the stewards and administrators of God's grace to the world around us.

As we ponder Christ's words—"I in them, and You in Me"—let us believe that just as the Father worked in Him, so Christ, the interceding High Priest, will work and pray in us.

As the faith of our high calling fills our hearts, we will begin to feel, quite literally, that nothing on earth compares for a moment with the privilege of being God's priests—walking continually in His holy presence, carrying the burden of souls to His throne, and receiving from His hand the power and blessing to pass on to others.

This is truly the fulfilment of the ancient word: "Man, created in the likeness and image of God."

TWENTY-FOURTH DAY
Intercession: The Link Between Heaven and Earth

"Thy will be done, as in heaven, so on earth."
—Luke 11:2

When God created heaven and earth, He intended heaven to be the divine pattern to which earth should be conformed. "As in heaven, so on earth" was meant to be the law of earth's existence.

This phrase "As in heaven, so on earth" invites us to consider what makes heaven glorious.

In heaven, God is all in all. Everything lives *in Him* and *for His glory*. And when we look at the world as it now is—with its sin and misery, with the vast majority having no true knowledge of God, and most who call themselves Christians for the most part still utterly indifferent to His claims while being estranged from His holiness and love —we feel how great a transformation is needed if the word is ever to be fulfilled: "As in heaven, so on earth."

And how will this ever come true?

Through the prayers of God's children.

Our Lord teaches us to pray for it.

Intercession is the great link between heaven and earth: the intercession of the Son, begun on earth, continued in heaven, and carried on by His redeemed people on earth. This will bring about the mighty change: "As in heaven, so on earth."

Just as Christ said, "I come to do Thy will, O God," and prayed in Gethsemane, "Thy will be done," so His redeemed ones— yielding themselves to His mind and Spirit —make His prayer their own and continually cry, "Thy will be done, as in heaven, so on earth."

Every parent's prayer for a child, every prayer for the salvation of the lost, or for greater grace for the saved, becomes part of the great unceasing cry rising day and night from the earth: "As in heaven, so on earth."

When God's children learn not only to pray for their immediate circles but also to enlarge their hearts to take in the whole Church and the whole world, then their united supplication will have power with God and hasten the day when it shall indeed be: "As in heaven, so on earth"— the whole earth filled with the glory of God.

Child of God, will you not yield yourself, like Christ, to live with this one prayer: "Father, Thy will be done on earth as in heaven"?

Prayer:

Our Father who art in heaven,
Hallowed be Thy Name.
Thy Kingdom come.
Thy will be done—as in heaven, so on earth.
Amen.

TWENTY-FIFTH DAY
The Fulfilment of God's Desires

"The Lord has desired Zion for His habitation.
Here will I dwell; for I have desired it."
—Psalm 132:13–14

Here we see God's huge desire, the desire that moved Him in the work of redemption: His heart longed to dwell with man and in man.

He said to Moses: "Let them make Me a sanctuary, that I may dwell among them."

Just as Israel had to prepare a dwelling place for God, so His children today are called to yield themselves for God to dwell in them, and to win others to become His dwelling place.

As God's desire toward us fills our hearts, it awakens in us the desire to gather others to become His dwelling place as well.

What an honor! What a high calling—to consider our earthly business as secondary, and to find our life and delight in winning souls in whom God may find His heart's pleasure: "Here will I dwell; for I have desired it."

And above all, this is something we can do through intercession. We can pray for those around us, asking God to give them His Holy Spirit.

It is God's plan that *man himself* should help build the dwelling place of God. It is in answer to the unceasing intercession of His children that He gives His power and His blessing.

As this great desire of God fills us, we will give ourselves fully to labor for its fulfilment.

Think of David. When he considered God's desire to dwell among Israel, he said:

"I will not give sleep to my eyes nor slumber to my eyelids until I find a place for the Lord, a habitation for the mighty God of Jacob."

And shall not we—who have been shown the far greater meaning of God's indwelling—give our lives for the fulfilment of His heart's desire?

Let us begin, more than ever before, to pray for our children, for the souls around us, and for the whole world—not only because we love them, but because God longs for them and God gives us the honor of being the channels through whom His blessing descends.

Children of God, awaken to the reality of what it means that God is seeking to train you as intercessors through whom the great desire of His loving heart may be fulfilled!

Prayer:

O God, who has said of human hearts, "Here will I dwell, for I have desired it," teach us, we pray, to pray day and night that the desire of Your heart may be fulfilled.
Amen.

TWENTY-SIXTH DAY
The Fulfilment of Man's Desire

"Delight thyself in the Lord; and He shall give thee the desires of thine heart."
—Psalm 37:4

God is love—an ever-flowing fountain from which streams an unceasing desire to make His creatures share in all the holiness and blessedness that are in Himself.

This desire for the salvation of souls is truly God's perfect will—His highest glory.

This loving desire of God—to gain His rightful place in the hearts of people—is given to all His children who are willing to yield themselves wholly to Him.

This is what it means to bear the likeness and image of God: to have a heart so filled with His love that we find our highest joy naturally in loving as He loves.

It is in this way that our text is fulfilled:

"Delight thyself in the Lord,"—delight in His own life of love— "and He will give thee the desires of thine heart."

Count on this: the intercession of love that rises to heaven will be met with the fulfilment of the desire of our heart.

We may be certain that as we delight in what God delights in, our prayers are inspired by Him and will be answered.

Then our prayer becomes: "Your desires, O my Father, are mine. Your holy will of love is my will too."

In fellowship with Him we gain the courage, with all our will and strength, to bring before Him the people and the circles that lie on our hearts—with a continually growing confidence that our prayer will be heard.

As we reach out in hearts that yearn, in yearning love, we take hold of God's will to bless, and we believe that He will work out His own gracious purpose in giving us the desire of our hearts—because the fulfilment of *His* desire has become the delight of our souls.

Thus we become, in the truest sense, God's fellow-laborers. Our prayer becomes part of God's divine work of reaching and saving the lost.

And we learn to find our happiness in losing ourselves for the salvation of those around us.

Prayer:

Our Father, teach us that only by delighting ourselves in You and in Your desires for people can we be inspired to pray rightly and be assured of answers.
Amen.

TWENTY-SEVENTH DAY
My Great Desire

"One thing have I desired of the Lord, that will I seek after:
  that I may dwell in the house of the Lord all the days of my life,
  to behold the beauty of the Lord, and to enquire in His temple."
—Psalm 27:4

Here we have man's response to God's desire to dwell within us. When God's longing toward us begins to govern our life and heart, our own desire becomes fixed on one thing: to dwell in the house of the Lord all the days of our life, to behold His beauty, to worship Him in the beauty of holiness.

And then, to enquire in His temple—to learn what it means when God says:

"I the Lord have spoken it, and I will do it.
  Yet I will be inquired of by the house of Israel to do it for them."

The more we realize God's loving desire to give His rest in our hearts, and the more our desire is stirred to dwell daily in His temple and look on, gaze at, understand and behold His beauty, the more the spirit of intercession will grow in us—so that we may claim all that God has promised in His New Covenant.

Whether we think of our Church and nation, our home and school, our near or wider circle—whether we consider the saved and all their needs, or the unsaved and their danger—the thought that God Himself longs to make His home and rest in human hearts, if only He is asked, will awaken our whole being from sleep. It will stir us to action. For Zion's sake we cannot keep silent.

All thoughts of our weakness or unworthiness will be swallowed up by the wonderful assurance that He has said of human hearts:

"This is My rest for ever;
 here will I dwell;
 for I have desired it."

As our faith grasps how high our calling is, and how essential is passionate, fervent, intense and persistent prayer is for the fulfilment of God's purpose, we will be drawn to give our lives to a closer walk with Him. We will be drawn to unceasing waiting upon Him.

We will be made a testimony to our brothers and sisters of what God is ready to do in them and in us.

Isn't it astonishing - incredible really - that God makes us partners in the accomplishment of His desires. That He commits His desires to our keeping, making it so that it is down to our own activity as to whether they are fulfilled or not?

Shame on us that we have not realized this enough!

Prayer:

Our Father in heaven, we earnestly ask You: give Your people, in power, the Spirit of grace and supplication—for Jesus' sake.
Amen.

TWENTY-EIGHTH DAY
Intercession Day and Night

"Shall not God avenge His own elect, which cry day and night unto Him, though He bear long with them?"
—Luke 18:7

When Nehemiah heard of the destruction of Jerusalem, he cried to God:
> "Hear the prayer of Thy servant, which I pray before Thy face day and night."

Of the watchmen set on the walls of Jerusalem, God said:
> "They shall never hold their peace day nor night."

And Paul wrote (1 Thessalonians 3:10, 13, R.V.):
> "Night and day praying exceedingly, to the end He may stablish your hearts unblameable in holiness before our God and Father."

Is such day-and-night prayer really needed—and is it really possible?

Yes—most certainly—it becomes possible when the heart has become so entirely possessed by a desire that it cannot rest until that desire is fulfilled.

It becomes possible when a person's life has come so fully under the power of the heavenly calling that nothing can prevent them from sacrificing everything for that desire's accomplishment.

When a child of God begins to see clearly a real vision of:

- the need of the Church and the world,
- the divine redemption God has promised in the outpouring of His love into our hearts,
- the power of true intercession to bring down the heavenly blessing,
- and the honor of being allowed, as an intercessor, to share in that work,

—then the surrendered believer naturally comes to regard this work as the most heavenly calling on earth: to cry day and night to God for the revelation of His mighty power.

Let us learn from David, who said: "The zeal of Thine house hath consumed me."

And from Christ our Lord, for whom these words were supremely true—that there is nothing so worth living for as this one thought: how to satisfy the heart of God in His longing for human fellowship and love, and how to win hearts to be His dwelling place.

We must refuse to give ourselves rest until we have made room for the Mighty One in our own hearts, and until we have devoted ourselves to the great work of intercession for those upon whom God's desires go out to.

May God so bring our hearts under the power of these divine truths that we truly yield ourselves to be devoted to Christ—and the longing to satisfy the heart of God is our main goal.

Prayer:

Lord Jesus, great Intercessor, who finds all Your glory in intercession, breathe, we pray, Your own Spirit into our hearts—for Your Name's sake.

Amen.

TWENTY-NINTH DAY
The High Priest and His Intercession

"We have such a High Priest... who is able to save them to the uttermost that come unto God by Him, seeing He ever liveth to make intercession for them."
—Hebrews 7:25–26; 8:1

There was a great difference between the high priest and the priests and Levites in Israel.

The high priest alone had access to the Holiest of All. He alone wore on his forehead the golden crown, "Holiness to the Lord." By his intercession on the Day of Atonement, he bore the sins of all the people.

The priests, on the other hand, offered the daily sacrifices, stood before the Lord, and came out to bless the people.

The distinction between high priest and

priest was great.

But greater still was the unity—they formed one body with the high priest, sharing with him the privilege of appearing before God to receive and administer His blessing to the people.

So it is with our great High Priest.

He alone has perfect power with God—in unceasing intercession—to obtain from the Father everything His people need.

And yet, though the distance between Him and the royal priesthood that surrounds Him is infinite, the unity and fellowship into which His people have been brought with Him is no less real.

The blessings He gets from the Father are meant for His people. His people receive these blessings when they fervently pray for them. After receiving them, they are supposed to share these blessings with the people around them, because God has placed them there to represent Him as His witnesses and representatives.

As long as Christians think merely of being saved—and of living a life that will make that salvation secure—they can never understand the mystery and power of intercession to which they are called.

But when they begin to understand that salvation is:

- a living union with Jesus Christ,
- an actual sharing of His life dwelling and working in us,
- a consecration of our whole being to live, labor, think, and will as a royal priesthood,

—then the Church will put on her strength and demonstrate, in fellowship with God and with people, how truly the likeness and power of Christ dwell in her.

If only God would open our hearts to know and experience what our royal priesthood is—to grasp the real meaning of living and praying in the name of Jesus, and believing that what we ask shall indeed be given!

Prayer:

O Lord Jesus, our Holy High Priest, breathe the spirit of Your own priesthood into our hearts.
Amen.

THIRTIETH DAY
A Royal Priesthood

"Call unto Me, and I will answer thee, and show thee great and mighty things which thou knowest not."
—Jeremiah 33:3

As you plead for the great mercies of the New Covenant to be given, keep these thoughts in mind:

1. God's infinite willingness to bless.
- His very nature is a pledge of this.
- He *delights* in mercy.
- He *waits* to be gracious.
- His promises—and the experience of His saints—assure us that He is eager to give.

2. Why is the blessing so often delayed?

In creating man with a free will and making him a partner in the rule of the earth, God chose to limit Himself.

He made Himself, in a sense, dependent

on what man would do.

Through prayer, *man determines the measure of what God can do in blessing.*

3. Think of how God is hindered from doing anything and disappointed when His children do not pray—or pray only a little.

The low, weak condition of the Church, the lack of power of the Holy Spirit for conversion and holiness—*all* of this is due to lack of prayer.

How different the Church and the unconverted world would be if God's people would take no rest in calling upon Him!

4. Yet God has blessed—up to the measure of His people's faith and zeal.

This is not a sign that we should be content. Rather, it should lead us to say: "If He has blessed our feeble prayers so much, what would He do if we yielded ourselves completely to a life of intercession?"

5. What a call to repentance—that our lack of dedication and being set apart for Him has kept back God's blessing from the world!

He was ready to save people, but we were not ready for the sacrifice of whole-hearted devotion to Christ and His service.

Children of God, He counts on you to take your place before His throne as intercessors.

Awake to your holy calling as a royal priesthood.

Begin to live a new life in the assurance that intercession—in likeness and fellowship with the Lord Jesus, who intercedes in heaven—is the highest privilege a person can desire.

Take up the promise with big expectations: "Call unto Me, and I will answer thee, and show thee great and mighty things which thou knowest not."

Let everyone who has read this far now answer before God whether he is willing—whether he longs—to give himself wholly to this blessed calling, and willing through the power of Jesus Christ to make intercession for the Church, God's people, and a dying world the chief object of his life.

Is this too much to ask? Is it too much to offer your life for the holy service of the royal priesthood— to the blessed Lord who gave Himself for us?

THIRTY-FIRST DAY
Intercession: A Divine Reality

"And another angel came... and there was given unto him much incense, that he should offer it with the prayers of all saints upon the golden altar which was before the throne."
—Revelation 8:3

The thoughts I've expressed in this book form a serious indictment on the low priority given to intercession in the teaching and practice of the Church—by both its ministers and members.

It is of supreme importance that intercession is an essential element of real Christian life. For those who take God's Word seriously, there can be no doubt this is true.

Intercession is, by astounding grace, an essential element in God's redeeming purpose—so essential that without it the failure of His work may, to some degree, lie at our door.

Christ's intercession in heaven is essential to completing the work He began on earth. But He also calls for the intercession of His saints to accomplish His purpose.

Think of what Scripture says: "All things are of God, who has reconciled us to Himself by Jesus Christ, and has given to us the ministry of reconciliation."

Just as reconciliation depended on Christ's faithfulness, so the completion of His work depends on the Church doing her part.

We see how Paul regarded day-and-night intercession as essential to fulfilling his God-given ministry.

Intercession is one expression of the mighty power of God working in His believing people.

Intercession is indeed a Divine reality. Without it, the Church loses:
- one of her chief beauties,
- the joy and the power of the Spirit-filled life,
- and the ability to accomplish great things for God.

Without it, the command to "preach the Gospel to every creature" can never be fulfilled.

Without it, the Church cannot rise from sickly and weak impotence to conquer the world.

And in the life of any believer—whether they are a minister or a member—there can be no entrance into the abundance and joy of daily fellowship with God except by taking one's place among God's elect— the watchmen and remembrancers of God, who cry to Him day and night.

Church of Christ, awake! Awake!

Listen to the call: "Pray without ceasing." Take no rest—and give God no rest.

Let your answer be—even if it begins with a sigh from deep within: "For Zion's sake, I will not hold my peace."

God's Spirit will reveal to us that a life of intercession is a divine reality—an essential, indispensable part of the great redemption, and therefore of the true Christian life.

May God help us to know and to fulfil our calling!

www.ingramcontent.com/pod-product-compliance
Lightning Source LLC
Chambersburg PA
CBHW022213090526
44584CB00013BA/838